50 Edible Activities for Parents and Children

Snacktivities!

MaryAnn F. Kohl and Jean Potter

Robins Lane Press
a division of Gryphon House, Inc.
www.robinslane.com

Library of Congress Cataloging-in-Publication Data

Kohl, Mary Ann F.
  Snacktivities! : 50 edible activities for parents and children /
  MaryAnn F. Kohl and Jean Potter.
    p. cm.
  ISBN 1-58904-010-4
    1. Cookery--Study and teaching (Elementary)--Activity programs.
2. Food presentation. I. Potter, Jean, 1947- II. Title.

TX661 .K66 2001
641.5'123--dc21

                                        2001041892

Cover and interior design by Bartko Design
Cover and interior illustrations by Lana Mullen

Published by Robins Lane Press
A division of Gryphon House
10726 Tucker St., Beltsville, MD 20704 U.S.A.
Copyright © 2001 by MaryAnn F. Kohl and Jean Potter
International Standard Book Number: 1-58904-010-4

To Larry Rood and Leah Curry-Rood, who have enriched my life.
MaryAnn F. Kohl

.

To my Aunt Rosell and Uncle Mark Benish.
Jean Potter

Contents

v

Snacktivities!

Souper Noodles

Ingredients

2 cups sifted flour, plus extra

1 pinch salt

3 large eggs

2 large cans clear chicken broth

Utensils

2 bowls

measuring cups and spoons

fork

wooden spoon

rolling pin

pot

kitchen cloth

paring knife

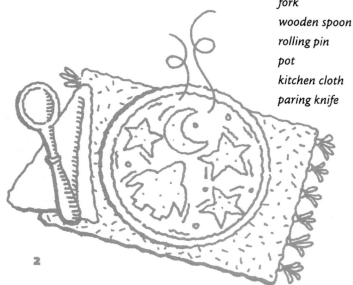

2

Process

1. Mix 2 cups of flour and a pinch of salt in a bowl. Set aside.
2. Crack the eggs into a separate bowl. Discard the shells. Lightly beat the eggs with a fork, then add to the bowl of flour and salt. Mix well with a wooden spoon.
3. When the flour mixture becomes too difficult to mix, begin working the mixture with your hands. Work until it forms a ball.
4. Sprinkle flour on the work surface and knead the noodle dough. If the dough is sticky, sprinkle with several tablespoons of flour. Knead until the dough is smooth and no longer sticky. Place it into a bowl and cover with a cloth. Let stand for 30 minutes.
5. Divide the noodle dough into egg-size balls. Rub a rolling pin with flour and add a little more flour to the work surface. Roll the noodle dough balls on the work surface to ¼-inch thickness.
6. Use the point of the paring knife to cut shapes out of the noodle dough sections. Score the shapes, then cut through the dough.
7. Pour the chicken broth into a pot. Place the soup on the stove and bring to a boil.
8. Add the shape-noodles to the soup. Simmer until the noodles are cooked—about 5 to 10 minutes.

Pain Décoré *(French: Decorated Bread)*

SERVES 4 OR MORE

Ingredients

frozen bread dough rolls (purchased
    bag of rolls, in balls)
beaten egg, in a cup
butter, jam, honey (optional)

Utensils

oven preheated to 350°F, or as directed
    on the frozen dough package
floured board
cookie sheet, coated with nonstick
    cooking spray
pastry brush
cup for egg
oven mitts

Note: Pain Décoré is
pronounced pan day'-cor-ay'

4

Process

1. Thaw the frozen dough balls as directed on the bag.
2. To design the bread, think of shapes that use circles, such as a flower with petals or a bunch of grapes. For this project, a bunch of grapes will be described, but feel free to make up any designs.
3. Place balls of dough on the greased cookie sheet in a grape pattern.
4. Pull a ball of dough into a thick stem shape and tuck it into the top of the grape design.
5. Pull another ball of dough and roll into a vine. Arrange the vine across the balls of dough.
6. Let the dough rise for 30 to 60 minutes. Brush beaten egg on the grape design with the pastry brush.
7. Bake the dough at 350°F for about 30 minutes, or as directed on the package. Wearing oven mitts, remove the bread when golden brown and hollow sounding when tapped with a knife handle.
8. Enjoy the Pain Décoré with butter, jam, honey or plain and warm from the oven. To eat, pull balls of baked bread from the larger grape design.

Make decorated bread by forming letters, leaves, flowers, birds, fish or any other design from the dough before baking. Brush with beaten egg before baking.

All-a-Round Rice Cake

Ingredients

large rice cake (one per person)

peanut butter

round foods, such as raisins, sliced carrots, sliced bananas

orange sliced in circles, to garnish

Utensils

spreading knife

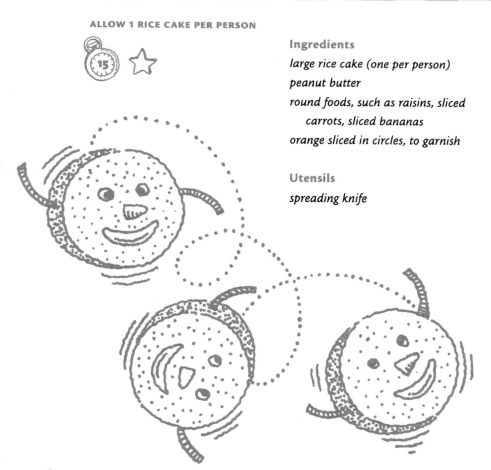

Process

1. Spread peanut butter on the rice cake with a knife.
2. Decorate the top of the rice cake circle with the circles of food, such as carrot circles, raisins or sliced bananas.
3. Garnish around the rice cakes with orange circles. Ta-da! A well-rounded lunch.

Pinwheel Sandwiches

ALLOW 1 TO 3 BREAD SLICES PER PERSON

Ingredients

slices of bread

sandwich spread, such as tuna salad, egg salad, cheese spreads, peanut butter, chicken salad, cinnamon sugar, apple butter, jam, cream cheese, cheese

variety of fresh vegetable slices, such as tomato slices, turnip slices, red, yellow and green pepper slices, carrot slices, celery slices, jicama slices, sliced mushrooms, sliced olives

Utensils

knife and cutting board

rolling pin

spreading knife

toothpicks

measuring spoon (one tablespoon)

plate

Process

1. Cut the crusts off the slices of bread with a knife.
2. Flatten each slice of bread with a rolling pin.
3. Spread one tablespoon of sandwich spread on each slice of bread.
4. Starting with one side, roll the bread jelly-roll fashion. Secure with a toothpick.
5. Slice the roll into circles or pinwheels and put on a plate.
6. Cut the cheese into different shapes.
7. Cut the vegetables into shapes and slices.
8. Arrange the bread pinwheels, cheese shapes and vegetable shapes on serving plates in pinwheel or spinner designs, or in any other designs.

Popcorn Sculpting

SERVES 4 TO 8

Ingredients

¼ cup margarine, plus 1 tablespoon
    extra
1 bag mini-marshmallows
12 cups popped popcorn
3 packages gelatin (such as Jell-O,
    4 serving size), different flavors
    and colors
choice of the following foods, such as
    bran sprouts, celery sticks, carrot
    slices

Utensils

3 bowls
oven mitts
wax paper or serving plate
large wooden spoon
large microwave-safe bowl
    or saucepan

Process

1. Place the margarine and the marshmallows in the microwave-safe bowl.
2. Microwave the two on high for 1½ to 2 minutes until the marshmallows are puffed.
3. Using oven mitts, remove the bowl of marshmallows from the microwave. Stir the mixture with a wooden spoon.
4. Divide the popcorn into three separate bowls.
5. Pour equal amounts of the marshmallow mixture over popcorn.
6. Sprinkle a different color of gelatin over each bowl of popcorn and marshmallow mixture.
7. Quickly stir with the spoon until the gelatin and marshmallow mixture evenly covers the popcorn mixture and let cool.
8. Rub some margarine on your hands. Take some of the popcorn mixture and mold into an interesting form. Add different colors of the popcorn mixture to make different parts of the sculpture.
9. Place the sculpture on wax paper or a serving plate. Add any of the remaining foods to make an interesting presentation of the sculpture just before serving.

Lemon Lights

SERVES 6 TO 8

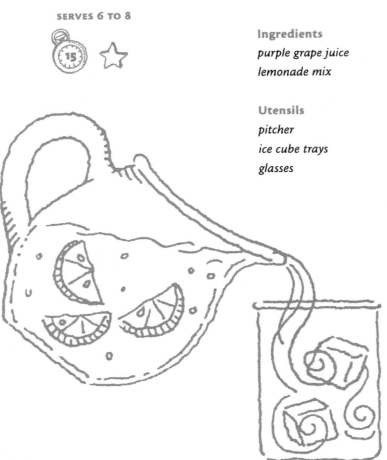

15

Ingredients
purple grape juice
lemonade mix

Utensils
pitcher
ice cube trays
glasses

Process

1. Fill each compartment of the ice cube trays with grape juice and place them in the freezer. Let them freeze overnight.
2. The next day, prepare the lemonade in the pitcher.
3. Remove the ice cubes from the freezer. Take the ice cubes out of the tray.
4. Place several ice cubes in each glass. Pour lemonade over the ice cubes.
5. While drinking, watch what happens to the colors in the lemonade.

Kaleidoscope Salad Plate

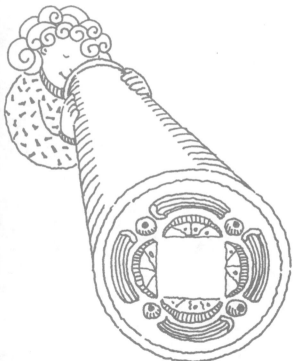

Ingredients
fresh vegetables, such as a firm
  tomato, carrot, celery
fresh or dried herbs, such as parsley,
  mint, celery leaves
fresh greens, such as lettuce,
  spinach, kale
optional foods, such as cheese
  slices, cold cuts
light vinegar and oil salad dressing

Utensils
kaleidoscope
cutting board and paring knife
clear glass plate or platter

*Look through a kaleidoscope
to see the designs made inside.
Notice the repeated patterns
in the circular design. The
repeating design will be a
theme in the salad recipe.*

Process

1. Slice the tomato into very thin slices on a cutting board.
2. Place the tomato slices on the clear glass platter in a circular design, similar to a pattern in a kaleidoscope.
3. Slice or tear an herb or green food into pieces. The pieces should resemble one another in size and shape. Add these herb pieces to the design, continuing the kaleidoscope pattern.
4. Add more slices, pieces and shapes of foods and place them in the circular kaleidoscope design on the plate.
5. Sprinkle the platter of vegetables with the light salad dressing. Chill for 30 minutes.
6. To serve, place the platter on a table and eat parts and pieces of the pattern, keeping the design intact as long as possible. For example, eat all the tomatoes first, then eat the parsley.

Place the platter on a glass table, lie down under the table, and look at the design. A sunny day will help the design look more like a kaleidoscope.

Polka Dot Party Melon

Ingredients

2 melons of contrasting colors, such
    as cantaloupe and honeydew
additional selection of fruits cut with a
    melon ball scoop, or circle-shaped
    fruits, such as raspberries, grapes,
    blueberries, strawberries (optional)

Utensils

knife and cutting board
hand towel
small melon ball scoop
2 bowls (or more if needed)
2 large plates or platters
spatula
salad plates

Process

1. Slice the two melons in half. Scoop out and discard the seeds and pulp. Cut away the skin from all four halves and discard. Dry hands on the hand towel to prevent slippery hands.

2. Place half of each melon upside down like domes on one large platter. Place the other two melon halves on the other platter.

3. Scoop one ball from the orange cantaloupe and place it in a bowl. Scoop one ball from a green honeydew and place it in the other bowl. Continue scooping balls from both halves and placing the balls in the bowls. Work carefully, keeping the melon halves intact.

4. When the halves are filled with holes, begin making the polka dot design. Take an orange melon ball and place it in a hole in the green melon. Then, take a green melon ball and place it in a hole in the orange melon. Fill all the holes with contrasting melon colors.

5. Scoop balls from other fruits and plug them into the melon holes too. Raspberries or grapes may fit right into the holes.

6. When all the holes are filled, follow the same procedure with the other two melon halves.

7. Serve the polka dot melons on platters for a cheerful, festive party snack. Guests can slice through the melon domes and serve themselves with a spatula on salad plates.

Snow White Snowflake

ALLOW 1 TORTILLA PER PERSON

Ingredients

package of flour tortillas
shredded mozzarella cheese
(or any white cheese such as
Monterey Jack or
white cheddar)

Utensils

kitchen scissors
baking sheet
oven mitts
spatula
preheated broiler or
toaster oven

Process

1. Fold the tortilla in half, and then in half again.
2. Cut out shapes and designs from the folded edges of the tortilla with the kitchen scissors. Cut through all of the layers, trying not to tear the tortilla.
3. Open the tortilla and place it flat on the baking sheet. It should resemble a snowflake design.
4. Carefully sprinkle the shredded mozzarella cheese on the snowflake tortilla. Try to keep the cheese away from the holes.
5. Place the baking sheet and snowflakes under the broiler or in the toaster oven just until the cheese bubbles. Watch carefully—it only takes a moment. Wearing oven mitts, remove the baking sheet from the oven. Set aside and let cool for a few minutes.
6. While waiting, sprinkle a little cheese on the white plate.
7. With a spatula, remove the tortilla snowflake from the baking sheet.
8. To serve, place the tortilla on a white plate. Sprinkle with a little more cheese, if desired.

Pretty Parfait

Ingredients

breakfast cereal

choice of nonfat yogurt in three
flavors, such as vanilla, strawberry,
lemon

choice of fruit in different colors, such
as raspberries, blueberries,
strawberries, grapes

Utensils

spoons

wide mouth glasses, one for each
parfait

spoon

ice tea spoons

20

Process

1. Place several spoons of one flavor of yogurt in a glass. Be sure to completely cover the bottom of the glass with the yogurt. Spread a little of the yogurt up the sides of the glass too.
2. Place a layer of breakfast cereal in the glass.
3. Add another flavor of yogurt on top of the cereal.
4. Arrange some fruit on the yogurt. When arranging the fruit pieces, hold the glass up and note the way they look from outside the glass. Press some against the sides of the glass.
5. Continue to layer the cereal, yogurt and fruit pieces.
6. Top off the glass with a piece or two of fruit to decorate.
7. Serve with an ice tea spoon for a colorful parfait dessert experience.

Veggie Bundles

ALLOW 1 BUNDLE PER PERSON

Ingredients
2 to 3 carrots
10 scallions
10 asparagus spears
10 green beans
bacon strips, precooked but not crispy

Utensils
vegetable peeler
4 paper plates
knife and cutting board
baking sheet
saucepans
oven mitts
spatula
oven preheated to 350°F
plates

> Counting vegetables
> in the bundles is part
> of the fun.

22

Process

1. Scrape the carrots with the vegetable peeler until they are clean. Trim both ends off of each carrot.
2. Cut the carrots into long strips (this can be difficult, so any strips are fine). Fill a saucepan nearly full with water and add the carrot strips.
3. Place the pan of carrots on the stove and bring to a boil for 2 minutes. Remove the carrots from the heat. Drain the water. Cool.
4. Put carrot strips on a paper plate.
5. Cook the green beans, asparagus and scallions in the same manner. Before cooking, trim both tips of the green beans and the root end of the asparagus. Use separate saucepans for each vegetable (or rinse saucepan before cooking each vegetable).
6. Place each vegetable variety on a separate paper plate.
7. Gather one of each of the vegetables into a bundle.
8. Wrap a bacon strip around the bundle and tie the ends in a knot. Place the bundles on the baking sheet.
9. Place the baking sheet in the preheated oven set at 350° and bake for 3 to 4 minutes, just until the bundles are thoroughly heated. Wear oven mitts and remove the bundles from the oven.
10. Transfer the Veggie Bundles with a spatula onto individual plates and serve!

Abacus Waffles

ALLOW 1 TO 2 WAFFLES PER PERSON

Ingredients

fresh assorted berries, such as
blueberries, raspberries,
blackberries, strawberries
box of frozen waffles
blueberry or other flavored syrup

Utensils

serving bowls
spoon
toaster
plates

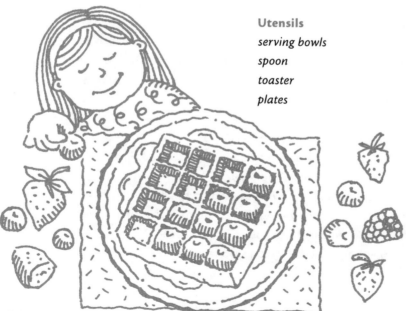

Process

1. Place the blueberries or other fresh berries in a serving bowl. Set aside.
2. Heat the frozen waffles in the toaster according to package directions. Remove waffles carefully and place them on a plate.
3. Look at the rows of holes or compartments in the waffles.
4. Place one berry in the first square in the first row.
5. Place two berries in the first two squares of the second row. (Create your own pattern by using different types of berries or alternating the berries and colors.)
6. Place three berries in the first three squares of the third row. Continue adding the blueberries according to the numbers until all the rows have some berries. Make as many waffles per person as desired.
7. Pour syrup on waffles before eating, if desired.

Berry designs can be made in any pattern in the waffle holes.

Cowpoke Cakes

SERVES 1 OR MORE

Ingredients

frozen pancake mix or homemade mix
4 tablespoons vegetable oil
butter, warm syrup or jam
fruit, optional

Utensils

electric skillet, griddle or large frying pan
spoon
clean squeeze bottle
large spoon
¼ cup measuring cup
spatula

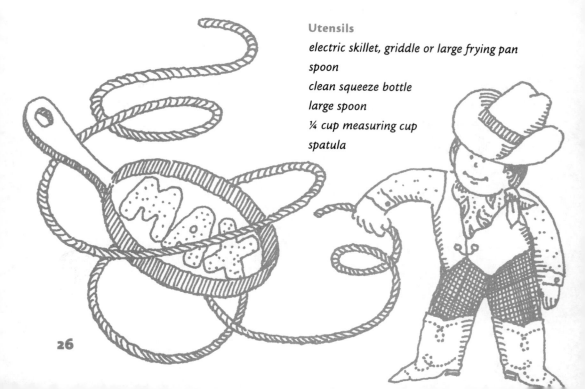

Process

1. Thaw out the frozen pancake batter.
2. Pour the oil into the electric skillet.
3. Turn the electric skillet on medium heat.
4. Spoon the pancake batter into the squeeze bottle. (This can be a very messy job.)
5. Squeeze the batter in the shape of a letter into the skillet.
6. When the letter has lightly browned on the bottom side, pour about ¼ cup of batter over the top of it. Cook the design cake until bubbles show and edges are dry.
7. Turn the cowpoke cake over to cook the other side.
8. Carefully remove the cowpoke cake from the skillet with the spatula.
9. Place the cowpoke cake on the serving plate with the design side showing. If desired, decorate the top of the cake with fruit. Serve with butter, warm syrup or jam.

Spell a word, name or message with pancakes. Create one letter for each pancake and then spread the cakes out on a plate or platter to be read and enjoyed.

ABC-heese Broil

SERVES 1 OR MORE

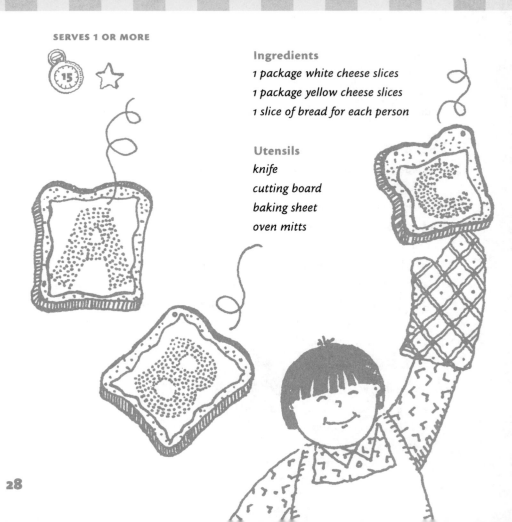

Ingredients
1 package white cheese slices
1 package yellow cheese slices
1 slice of bread for each person

Utensils
knife
cutting board
baking sheet
oven mitts

Process

1. Select a word (or letter) to place on the sandwich.
2. Place one slice of white cheese on the bread.
3. Place the yellow cheese on the cutting board work surface and cut out letters with a sharp knife.
4. Peel the letters out of the cheese. Spell the word by placing the letters on the white cheese that is on the bread.
5. Place the slice of bread on the baking sheet.
6. Turn the oven on broil. Place the baking sheet under the broiler for a few minutes until the cheese melts. Watch carefully so the cheese does not burn. Wear oven mitts and remove the baking sheet from the oven.
7. Place the cheese sandwich on a plate to serve.

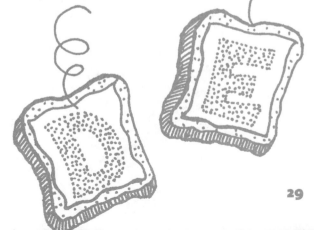

Sentence Sandwiches

ALLOW 1 SLICE OF BREAD PER PERSON

Ingredients
fruit jelly
sliced bread
alphabet cereal

Utensils
plates
spreading knife

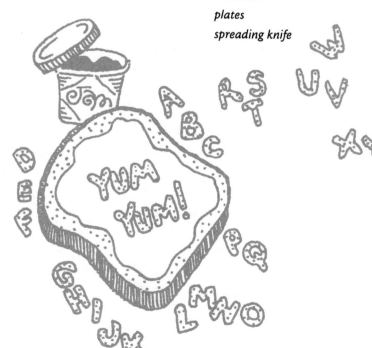

Process

1. Place a slice of bread on each plate.
2. Spread the fruit jelly on each slice of bread.
3. Spread a handful of the cereal on a plate.
4. Select the appropriate letters to form initials, words and simple sentences.
5. Place the letters on the bread slices, forming sentences and/or even a secret message!

Tomato Tower

SERVES 2 TO 4

Ingredients

2 firm, large tomatoes

sliced cheese

shredded lettuce (optional)

spreads, such as

   cream cheese or vegetable dip

   (optional)

Utensils

knife

paper towels

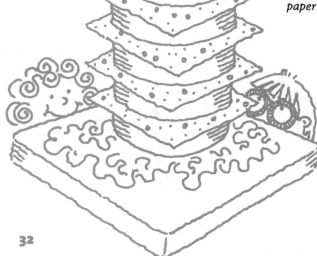

Process

1. Slice the tomatoes horizontally into at least four slices. Save the top and bottom of one tomato. (See the illustration.)
2. Place tomato slices on a paper towel for 5 minutes to drain the moisture.
3. Find the bottom part of the tomato and place it on the plate.
4. Place one slice of cheese on the sliced side of the bottom tomato.
5. Select a tomato slice and place it on top of the cheese.

Add layers of the optional spreads too, if desired.

6. Place another cheese slice on top of this tomato slice.
7. Place another tomato slice on top of the cheese.
8. Continue building the tomato tower until all of the tomato slices are used.
9. Spread the lettuce around the bottom of the tomato and serve. The tower can be eaten with a knife and fork, or pulled apart and eaten with fingers.

Build-It Party Sandwich

Ingredients

¼ cup margarine

⅛ teaspoon salt

1 tablespoon lemon juice

3 ounces cream cheese

5 thin slices of natural white bread

10 thin slices of whole grain bread

20 thin tomato slices

20 thin cucumber slices

Utensils

medium mixing bowl and spoon

small round biscuit cutter or
    cookie cutter

knife and cutting board

spreading knife

toothpicks

wax paper

teaspoon

34

Process

1. Mix together the margarine, salt, lemon juice and cream cheese in a bowl. Set aside.

2. With the small round cookie cutter, cut four circles from each white bread slice (20 total), and four circles from each whole wheat slice (40 total).

3. Using the same cutter, cut one circle from each tomato and cucumber slice. Use the scraps of vegetables for other salad recipes. Use the bread scraps to feed the birds, make croutons or make bread stuffing.

4. Spread ½ teaspoon cream cheese mixture on both sides of each white bread circle and set aside on wax paper. Spread cheese mixture on one side of each wheat circle.

5. To assemble the small stacked sandwich, follow this pattern: wheat bread, tomato, white bread, cucumber, wheat bread.

6. Poke each stack with a toothpick to secure, and serve as party or lunch sandwiches.

Little Log Buildings

Ingredients

⅓ cup peanut butter

3 tablespoons honey

½ cup crushed corn flakes

½ cup quick oatmeal

¼ cup dry milk

chocolate sprinkles

Utensils

measuring cups and spoons

mixing bowl

wooden spoon

baking sheet

Process

1. Place the peanut butter and honey in a mixing bowl and mix well with the wooden spoon.
2. Add the corn flakes, oatmeal and dry milk and mix well to form dough.
3. Pinch off a small amount of the dough mixture.
4. Roll the small amount of dough into 2-inch-long by ½-inch-wide logs.
5. Place the sprinkles on the baking sheet.
6. Roll the logs in sprinkles.
7. Stack the logs on a plate on top of one another to form a building.
8. Serve the building as a yummy dessert.

Banana Boats

Ingredients

bananas

lemon juice in a small cup, at least 2
    tablespoons

any choices of favorite fruits, such as
    watermelon, cantaloupe,
    strawberries, pineapple, berries,
    apple slices

Utensils

knife and cutting board

spoon

pastry brush

sandwich pick or toothpick with
    paper sail, optional

38

Process

1. Place the unpeeled banana on the cutting board so it curves upright like a boat.
2. Find the natural ridges of the banana.
3. Cut a long slice down one side on the inside curve of the banana, around the end and up the other side of the banana with a knife (but not all the way through the banana). This cut forms a large hole in the curved side of the banana. (See the illustration.)
4. Peel the cut-out section only, not the whole banana.
5. Scoop out some of the banana inside.
6. Dip the pastry brush into the lemon juice and paint the inside of the banana with lemon juice to prevent it from turning brown.
7. Cut favorite fruits into designs, sections and shapes. Arrange the fruits inside the banana boats like people and cargo riding inside.
8. Add a sandwich pick with a paper sail, if desired.

Sail away to snack time!

Sailboat Eggs

ALLOW 1 EGG PER SAILOR

Ingredients

hard-boiled eggs

1 teaspoon mayonnaise

½ teaspoon mustard

1 cup diced green peppers

carrot sticks

celery sticks

chopped pimentos

lettuce leaves

Utensils

knife and cutting board

bowl

fork

spoon

toothpicks for mast

scissors

paper for sails

tape

Process

1. Peel the hard-boiled eggs. Discard shells.
2. Cut the eggs in half lengthwise.
3. Remove the yolks and place them in a bowl.
4. Mash the yolks with the mayonnaise and mustard.
5. Spoon the mixture back into the egg white sections.
6. Decorate the egg sections with the celery sticks, carrot sticks and chopped pimentos.
7. Cut the paper into sails, attach to the toothpicks with tape and put into eggs.
8. Place the lettuce on a serving plate, then put the eggs on top of the lettuce.

Trees in Snow

Ingredients

½ cup cottage cheese

broccoli florets, precooked, steamed
    lightly or raw

1 tablespoon Italian dressing

Utensils

measuring cup and tablespoon

small dish

fork

Process

1. Spread the cottage cheese in a thick layer in the small dish.
2. Arrange the broccoli florets so they stand in the cottage cheese, resembling trees in the snow.
3. Drizzle a little Italian dressing over the broccoli florets to flavor the salad.
4. Serve the Trees in Snow with a fork as a healthy, tasty salad.

Cherry Tomato Blossoms

SERVES 5 TO 10

Ingredients

½ pound cherry tomatoes
¾ cup low-fat cream cheese
1 package dry salad dressing mix
   (any flavor)
cucumber
fresh parsley sprigs
scallions or green onions
Romaine lettuce

Utensils

knife and cutting board
small spoon or demitasse spoon
paper towels
small mixing bowl and spoon
pastry bag with small star tip
fork

Process

1. Cut off cherry tomato tops with a knife. Discard the tomato tops or add to the compost pile. Carefully scoop out the insides of the cherry tomatoes with a small spoon.

2. Place the empty tomatoes upside down on a double thickness of paper towels to drain.

3. Mix the cream cheese and dry salad dressing in a small bowl. Then, put the cheese mixture in a pastry bag fitted with a small star tip.

4. Squeeze the cheese mixture into the tomato cavities. Fill all the tomatoes.

5. Scrape the prongs of a fork straight down the sides of a cucumber to etch lines in the skin. Slice the cucumbers into ¼ or ⅛ -inch slices.

6. Arrange 3 or 4 cucumber slices on a serving plate. Place one tomato on top of each cucumber slice to look like the blossom of a flower.

7. Place the parsley sprigs in the cheese-stuffed tomato to resemble leaves of a flower.

8. Arrange several green onions or scallions on the serving plate with bottom sections together and tops fanning out to resemble stems of flowers.

9. Set a tomato flower at the top of each scallion. Arrange the Romaine lettuce leaves near the scallions to look like leaves growing from a stem.

Biscuit Blossoms

Ingredients

spinach leaves

refrigerator biscuits (or your favorite
biscuit recipe)

choice of fruits and nuts, such as
strawberries, blueberries,
raspberries, blackberries, apple
slices, apricots, almonds

Utensils

oven preheated to 375°F or according
to biscuit directions

paper towels

baking sheet

oven mitts

kitchen scissors

spatula

Process

1. Wash the spinach leaves under running water and pat dry with paper towels. Set aside until later.

2. Open the package of biscuits and separate the biscuits from the roll. Snip tiny cuts around the edge of each biscuit with kitchen scissors to form flower petals, or
   - cut biscuits in half and press them into flower shapes
   - join several biscuits or pieces of biscuits together into a flower shape
   - form the dough into shapes by hand

3. Place the biscuit blossoms about 2 inches apart on the baking sheet. Use a finger to press a dent in the biscuit where pieces of fruit or nuts will be placed. Place several pieces in the indentation in each biscuit.

4. Bake the biscuits for about 10 minutes at 375° or until lightly golden brown. Wear oven mitts and remove the biscuits from the oven. Cool a little.

5. Remove the Biscuit Blossoms from the baking sheet with a spatula and arrange them on the serving tray.

Banana Tree

ALLOW 1 BANANA TREE PER PERSON

Ingredients

lettuce leaf
pineapple ring
banana
sliced fruits, such as grapes, cut up
        pears, cherries, cut up peaches
strawberries or other berries
apple slices or chunks
cheese, cut in cubes

Utensils

knife and cutting board
toothpicks
salad plate

Process

1. Place a lettuce leaf on the salad plate.
2. Place a pineapple ring on the lettuce leaf.
3. Peel the banana and cut it in half.
4. Stand the cut end of the banana half in the center of the pineapple to resemble a tree trunk.
5. Place a toothpick through a selected piece of fruit.
6. Stick the other end of the toothpick into the top area of the banana. Each toothpick with a piece of fruit will represent a branch on the banana tree.
7. Fill the tree with as many fruit branches as desired. It may be necessary to hold the banana with one hand so it does not tip over when first beginning the work.
8. The banana trees can be served as fruit salad to be eaten with the fingers.

Apple Saturn Biscuit Circles

Ingredients
baking mix, such as Bisquick
1 apple, unpeeled
butter (optional)

Utensils
oven preheated to 425°F or
*   according to baking*
*   directions*
rolling pin
doughnut cutter
small melon ball scoop
baking sheet
oven mitts

Process

1. Prepare biscuits according to the package directions.
2. Roll out the biscuit dough with a rolling pin.
3. Cut the biscuits with a special "doughnut cutter." A doughnut cutter has a ring with a hole in the center.
4. Put the "doughnut" biscuits on a baking sheet.
5. Push the melon ball scoop into the apple and turn to scoop out apple balls.
6. Place an apple ball in the hole of each biscuit.
7. Place the apple biscuits in the oven and bake according to package directions, usually about 8 minutes.
8. When they are baked, wear oven mitts and remove from the oven. Cool for a few minutes.
9. Place the apple biscuits on a serving plate. Serve with butter, if desired.

51

Erupting Lava Apple

ALLOW 1 APPLE PER PERSON

Ingredients
1 apple per person
¼ cup peanut butter per apple
⅛ cup dried fruit bits or seeds, such as raisins, sunflower seeds, dried mixed fruits, popcorn

Utensils
apple corer
small bowls
butter knife

Process

1. Remove the core of the apple with the apple corer.
2. Mix the peanut butter and the fruit bits or seeds in one of the small bowls. Stir them together with a butter knife.
3. Fill the hole in the apple with the peanut butter and fruit bits mixture.
4. Sprinkle more fruit or seeds on top of the peanut butter.
5. Eat the lava apple for a snack. The lava will erupt and spread over your chin and face. Napkins will help keep the lava under control.

The recipe also works well with softened cheddar cheese

Monster Face Salad

Ingredients

lettuce

about 1 cup cottage cheese

selection of favorite fresh, raw
*   vegetables, such as cherry*
*   tomatoes, alfalfa sprouts, green*
*   bell, pepper slices, olives, broccoli,*
*   red bell pepper slices, zucchini*
*   slices, peas, beans*

Utensils

plate

ice-cream scoop

Process

1. Place a lettuce leaf on a plate.
2. Place a scoop of cottage cheese on the lettuce with the ice-cream scoop.
3. Decorate the cottage cheese with the vegetables to design a scary face, animal or design.
4. Serve immediately or place in the refrigerator until serving time as a salad or light lunch.

This recipe can be doubled or extended easily to serve more people. It is also delicious when made with fruit instead of vegetables.

Me and My Shadow Toast

Ingredients

6 slices day-old bread

4 large eggs

3 tablespoons milk

3 tablespoons butter

choose any toppings, such as jam,
    fruit syrup, maple syrup, fresh berries,
    raisins, peanut butter, brown sugar,
    currants

powdered sugar

Utensils

serving plate

oven preheated to 150°F

people-shaped cookie cutters or
    sharp knife

shallow dish

whisk

wide frying pan

cooking fork

spatula

oven mitts

Process

1. Put a serving plate in the oven to keep warm for later.

2. Place the bread on the work surface. Press a people-shaped cookie cutter into the bread or cut out a person from the bread with a sharp knife.

3. Remove the cookie cutter and take the people shape out of the bread, keeping both the shape and the outline intact. Set aside. Save the scrap outline of bread.

4. Crack open four eggs into the shallow dish. Discard the shells. Add 3 tablespoons of milk to the eggs and whisk together.

5. Put the butter in the frying pan. Warm over medium heat to melt.

6. Dip the people shapes in the egg mixture, coating each side. Then, place the egg-coated people shapes in the warm pan and cook them on each side until golden brown. Transfer the people shapes with a spatula from the pan to the warm serving plate. Leave in the warm oven.

7. Next, coat the bread scrap outlines with egg and cook them to make Shadow Toast. For additional fun, pour some of the egg mixture into the frame of the Shadow Toast to fill the hole. Cook on one side, and then using the spatula, turn to cook the other side until brown.

8. When the French toast is cooked, place the shadows on the warm serving plate with the people. Wearing oven mitts, place the plate with Me and My Shadow Toast on the table. Each person can add toppings to their toast to decorate it and to make it even more delicious and friendly.

Mix 'n Match Sandwich Faces

ALLOW 2 HALVES PER PERSON

Ingredients

two kinds of bread, such as wheat, white, sourdough, rye

choice of sandwich spreads, such as egg salad, tuna salad, peanut butter, cheese

choice of additional foods for decorating and facial features, such as raisins, carrot pieces, green pepper pieces, celery slices, egg slices, almonds, seeds, olives, mushroom slices, cheese shapes, radish slices, apple pieces, parsley leaves, lettuce

mustard

ketchup

Utensils

tools to cut or design foods for decorations, such as knife, small circle cutter, vegetable peeler, apple corer

toothpicks

fork

serving tray

Process

1. Choose two pieces of bread for each sandwich.

2. Slice each piece of bread in half, making a rectangle or a semi-circle. Spread a sandwich filling on the bread. Top with the other piece of bread.

3. Select from the decorating foods to design eyes and nose on the top half of the sandwich by pressing foods into the bread. In the same way, design a mouth on the other half of the sandwich for the lower part of the face (sandwich).

4. For fun, first place all the eye and nose sandwich halves on a serving tray in a line. Then, place the mouth sandwich halves beneath each eye and nose half, but do not match the bread types. Place miss matched halves together so the faces will be all mixed up.

5. Everyone chooses a top half and a bottom half that they like that matches or does not match and places it on their own sandwich plate. What a crazy, mixed-up lunch!

Start with a round piece of bread. Cut a circle out with a cookie cutter or a large mouth jar!

Scary Eyeballs

SERVES 6 TO 12

Ingredients

6 hard-boiled eggs
2 tablespoons mayonnaise
1 tablespoon prepared mustard
1 tablespoon sweet pickle relish
¼ teaspoon salt
6 black or green olives
alfalfa sprouts

Utensils

knife and cutting board
medium bowl
fork
spoon
1 Styrofoam egg carton, washed with
   soapy water and dried

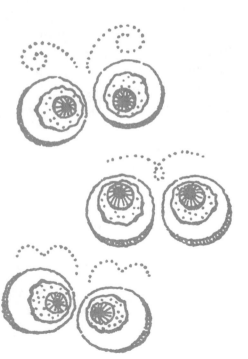

Process

1. Crack open a hard-boiled egg. Peel the shell from the egg.
2. Cut the egg in half the short way, across the middle, not from end to end.
3. Remove cooked yolk from the egg and place it in the bowl. Crack, peel and cut the other hard-boiled eggs.
4. Mash all the yolks with a fork. Add mayonnaise, mustard, pickle relish and salt to the yolks and mix well.
5. Spoon yolk mixture into each egg white half to resemble an eyeball.
6. Slice each olive in half with a knife.
7. Place an olive on top of each egg to resemble the pupil and iris of an eye.
8. Stuff each egg carton compartment with alfalfa sprouts. Place an eyeball on top of the sprouts in each egg carton compartment.
9. To serve, place the egg carton on the table so guests can select eyeballs to munch.

Smiley Snack

SERVES 2 TO 5

Ingredients

1 to 5 red apples

peanut butter

choice of food items for "teeth," such as miniature marshmallows, berries, raisins

Utensils

knife and cutting board

spreading knife

Hee Hee

Ha Ha

HoHo

Process

1. Cut the apple into quarters with a knife.
2. Cut each quarter in half again to make two thin slices for each "smile."
3. Spread peanut butter on one side of each thin smiley-slice to act as an adhesive glue.
4. Choose the foods that will be the teeth of the smile. Arrange the teeth foods—marshmallows, berries, raisins, other foods or any combination of them—on the peanut butter.
5. Assemble the second apple slice with the peanut butter slice facing down on top of the first slice and the "teeth." This forms a mouth with teeth inside.
6. Serve the smiley faces on a cheerful plate as a snack.
7. Read funny books or tell funny jokes while eating.

Dinosaur Claws

SERVES 5

Ingredients

1 can of refrigerator biscuits

margarine, melted

cinnamon sugar

almond slivers

Utensils

oven preheated to 425°F or according to biscuit
    directions

baking sheet

pastry brush

oven mitts

squares of clean, plain cardboard

permanent markers

64

Process

1. Bake the biscuits according to package directions, usually about 8 to 10 minutes.
2. Wear oven mitts and remove the baking sheet and biscuits from the oven.
3. Brush each biscuit with melted margarine. Sprinkle biscuits with cinnamon sugar.
4. While the biscuit is still very warm, carefully insert 5 almond slivers around the edge of the biscuit so it looks like the claws of a dinosaur.
5. Draw tracks near the edges on the clean squares of cardboard with the permanent markers.
6. Serve the claws on the cardboard squares.

Bunny Pears

Ingredients

1 can pear halves

lettuce leaves

selection of foods, such as toasted
 almonds, strawberries, raisins,
 blueberries

squirt can of whipped cream,
 (optional)

Utensils

can opener

strainer

plate

66

Process

1. Open the can of pears with a can opener.
2. Place the pear halves into a strainer to drain over the sink.
3. Arrange the lettuce leaves on a plate.
4. Place the pear halves, rounded side up, on the lettuce leaves.
5. Use the remaining ingredients to add features to each pear to make it into a bunny.
6. If desired, just before serving, squirt a whipped cream tail on the bunny.

Prehistoric Eggs

Ingredients
4 to 6 eggs
cool water
1 tablespoon food coloring (choose
    more than one color if desired)
lettuce

Utensils
saucepan
bowl
spoon

Process

1. Place the eggs in a saucepan filled with cool water on the stove.
2. Bring the eggs to a boil over medium heat. Turn heat down and gently simmer the eggs for 8 to 10 minutes. Then, remove pan from heat.
3. Fill a bowl with cool water. Add several drops of food coloring to the water and mix. For more than one color, add drops of food coloring to several bowls of water.
4. Put the eggs in the bowl of colored water, or a few eggs in each bowl of different colored water.
5. One at a time, lift each egg out of the water and carefully crack the shells all over with the back of a spoon. Do not peel any of the eggshell off yet.
6. Return the eggs to the colored water until cool.
7. Next, take the eggs out of the water with the spoon. Peel the cracked eggs.
8. Place the lettuce in the serving bowl to resemble grass or weeds. Place the prehistoric eggs on the lettuce to serve.
9. Eat as a snack or part of a meal.

Banana Snake

SERVES 1 TO 2

Ingredients

lettuce

peanut butter

chow mein noodles

banana

raisins

sprinkles, bread crumbs, small candies

Utensils

plates

table knife

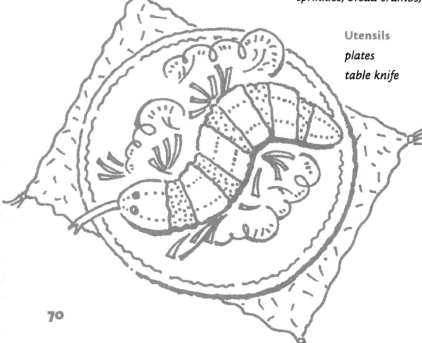

Process

1. Tear a lettuce leaf into small pieces and place on a plate.
2. Slice the banana into ½-inch chunks.
3. Smear peanut butter on the cut sides of the banana chunks.
4. Place the peanut buttery banana slices in a row on the plate. Add the ends of the bananas to form the ends of the snake. The sections will stick together with the peanut butter.
5. Place small dabs of peanut butter where the eyes and spots are on the snake. Add raisins as the eyes, etc.
6. Decorate the snake by sticking on other ingredients using the peanut butter.
7. Enjoy as an entertaining snack or dessert.

Fluffy Breakfast Nest

SERVES 1 TO 2

Ingredients

2 slices bread
butter
2 eggs
salt and pepper

Utensils

toaster
oven preheated to 350°F
oven mitts
butter knife
baking sheet
2 bowls
electric mixer
spoon
spatula

Process

1. Place two slices of bread in a toaster and toast very lightly.
2. Spread butter on the toast with a butter knife. Place the buttered toast on the baking sheet. Set aside.
3. Crack each egg and let the whites fall into a bowl. Then, put the yolks into a separate bowl. Be careful not to break the yolks.
4. Beat the egg whites with the electric mixer until they form stiff pointed peaks.
5. Spoon egg whites onto each slice of toast. Take the spoon and form a dent in the center of the egg white mound to make nest pockets.
6. Carefully spoon one egg yolk into each egg white dent.
7. Place the baking sheet with toast and eggs in the oven and bake until the whites turn brown and the yolks are cooked through, usually about 4 minutes.
8. Wear oven mitts and remove the baking sheet from the oven.
9. Place the nests on a plate with a spoon or spatula to serve.

Spider Sandwiches

Ingredients

2 slices wheat sandwich bread per
    person
sandwich spread, such as
    peanut butter, tuna salad, soft
    cheese
½ can cheese curls or pretzel sticks
raisins

Utensils

cookie cutter, 2½ inch round
plain paper plates
black permanent marker

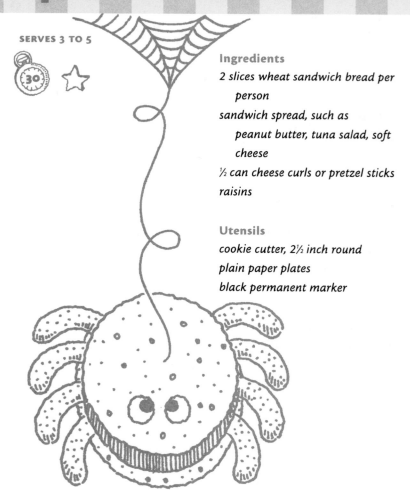

74

Process

1. Place the bread slices on the work surface. Cut a circle from each bread slice with the cookie cutter.
2. Divide the bread circles into two equal piles.
3. Spread about two tablespoons of sandwich spread on all of the bread circles in one pile.
4. Press eight cheese curls or pretzel sticks in the sandwich spread half way around each circle to make the legs of the spider.
5. Place the remaining bread circle on top of the sandwich spread-coated circles.
6. Using a finger, poke two small indentations on top of each sandwich. Push one raisin into each indentation to make the eyes.
7. Draw a spider web with the permanent black marker on the edges of a paper plate. Place one spider on each plate and serve for a silly lunch.

Flutterby Sandwiches

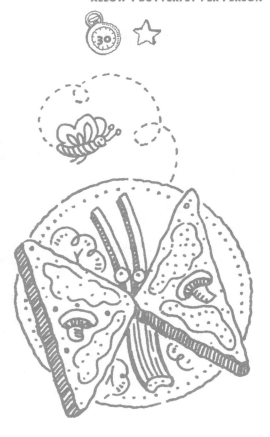

ALLOW 1 BUTTERFLY PER PERSON

Ingredients

1 large package cream cheese
2 slices white bread per person
food coloring or fruit juice
choices or variety of small food items, such
   as olives, dried fruit bits, raisins, celery
   bits, carrot sticks, mushroom slices
1 Romaine lettuce leaf per person

Utensils

knife and cutting board
small bowls, one for each color
small spoons, one for each color
butter knives, one for each color

Process

1. Cut the cream cheese block into 3 or 4 equal parts with a knife.

2. Place each section of cream cheese in a small bowl. Add 1 drop of food coloring or fruit juice to each bowl. Each bowl will have a different color.

3. Mix the food coloring (or juice) and cream cheese with a spoon until well blended. Use a different spoon for each color. Set aside.

4. Cut the bread in half diagonally with a knife to create two butterfly wings.

5. Place the two points of the butterfly wings together on the work surface. (See the illustration.)

6. Spread the colored cream cheese on the wings with butter knives to make colors and patterns.

7. Add additional decoration with food pieces to create antennae and any other butterfly features, real or imagined.

8. Place a Romaine lettuce leaf on the plate to give the butterfly a place to show off its wings. Place the butterfly on the leaf. Serve as a snack or lunch.

Jack Frost Treat

SERVES 6

Ingredients

4 cups confectioners' sugar

3 tablespoons meringue powder
(available at kitchen supply stores)

6 tablespoons warm water

edible glitter or decorative sugar
sprinkles

Utensils

baking sheet

wax paper

large bowl

electric mixer

pastry bag with number 10 point

paintbrush

spatula

nylon thread (optional)

Process

1. Cover the baking sheet with wax paper. Set aside.
2. Place the confectioners' sugar, meringue powder and water in the large bowl. Beat the sugar mixture on low speed with the electric mixer until well mixed. Turn the electric mixer up to high and beat the mixture for up to 7 minutes or until stiff peaks form.
3. Spoon the sugary meringue into the pastry bag.
4. Make snowflake designs, each about the size of a walnut, on the wax paper-covered baking sheet. Draw a line first, then make lines over top of the first one. Add curls, circles, triangles and different shapes that resemble a snowflake.
5. Dip the paintbrush in water and very lightly paint water over each snowflake. Sprinkle the glitter or sugar sprinkles over the snowflakes before the water dries.
6. Let the snowflakes dry.
7. Carefully remove the snowflakes from the wax paper with a spatula.
8. Snowflakes (or any other shape) may also be used to garnish or decorate cakes, cupcakes or other wintry recipes, and they are delicious to eat at any time.
9. Very carefully, tie a thread to each snowflake and hang, if desired.

79

Valentine Wigglers

SERVES 2 TO 4

Ingredients
4 small packages red gelatin, such as
    Jell-O
2½ cups boiling water
whipped topping, thawed
bits of fresh fruits or nuts for garnish,
    such as apple, strawberry, banana,
    raspberries, almonds, ground
    walnuts

Utensils
large glass measuring cup-mixing bowl
measuring cup
rubber spatula or scraper for stirring
rectangular pan
plastic knife
spoon
pastry bag

Process

1. Pour the four boxes of red gelatin into a large glass measuring cup-mixing bowl that has a handle and pouring spout.

2. Add the boiling water to the gelatin and stir the mixture slowly with the rubber spatula until the gelatin completely dissolves. Scrape the sides of the bowl while stirring so all the granules are dissolved. Pour the gelatin into the rectangular pan. (Don't be surprised if there are spills.)

3. Place the pan of gelatin in the refrigerator and let it chill until it is firm, usually for several hours. When chilled and firm, remove the pan from the refrigerator.

4. To loosen the gelatin from the pan, dip the bottom of pan in a sink filled with 2 inches of warm water for a few seconds. Set the pan of gelatin on the work surface again.

5. Trace a large heart shape or pattern in the gelatin. Cut the line with a knife.

6. Carefully—and with two or more hands—lift the heart out of pan and place it on a serving plate.

7. Next, spoon some thick whipped topping into the pastry bag. Squeeze the bag gently to make designs or to write on the gelatin heart. Decorate around the heart too, if desired. Garnish with bits of fresh fruits or nuts.

8. The leftover gelatin can be cut with small cookie cutters or cut into cubes with a knife to further decorate the heart dessert. Or, the leftovers can be nibbled now or enjoyed later.

Flower Fruit Bread

Ingredients

favorite bread, such as
*   English muffin, banana bread,*
*   biscuit or bagel, sandwich bread*
ricotta cheese or cottage cheese
fresh fruits, such as kiwi, grapes,
*   strawberries, peaches, raspberries,*
*   blueberries*

Utensils

spreading knife
knife and cutting board

Process

1. Spread any favorite bread with the ricotta or cottage cheese.
2. Slice the fruits into small pieces.
3. Decorate the bread with the fruits to make flower burst designs or other designs. See illustration.
4. Eat and enjoy this simple, delicious snack or light breakfast.

Frozen Juice Cubes

SERVES 8 TO 10

Ingredients

*favorite summer beverage(s), such as
fruit juice, lemonade, fruit drink,
sparkling juices*

*maraschino or mint cherry, one for
each glass*

*thin slices of favorite citrus fruit(s),
such as lime, orange, grapefruit,
lemon*

water or other summer drink

*optional drink garnishes, such as fruit
kabob on a toothpick, nontoxic
flower, paper umbrella*

Utensils

ice cube trays

tall, cold glasses

straw or swizzle stick, optional

Process

1. Fill one ice cube tray with a summer beverage or juice.
2. Place one cherry in each section of another ice cube tray and add water.
3. Place both trays in the freezer until solid.
4. Chill fruits in the refrigerator.
5. Serve a favorite summer drink or ice water with the colored ice cubes, cherry ice cubes and thin fruits floating in the drink or perched on the rim of the glass.
6. Add a straw, a swizzle stick, a fruit kabob, paper umbrella or a flower to make the beverage even fancier, if desired.

Serve with a spoon to avoid choking hazards.

Firecracker Sandwiches

SERVES 8

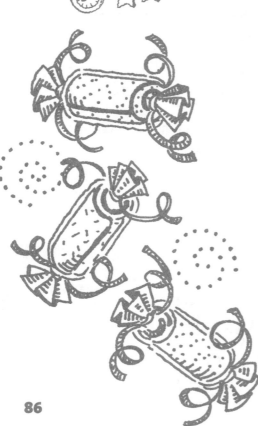

Ingredients

1 13-ounce can chunk light tuna packed
   in water, drained
⅓ cup mayonnaise
¼ teaspoon salt
1 medium-size carrot, peeled and grated
¼ cup dark raisins
8 slices firm white bread with
   crusts
   removed
lemonade, optional

Utensils

mixing bowl and spoon
rolling pin
colored plastic wrap
twist-ties or colorful ribbons

Process

1. Place the tuna, mayonnaise and salt in the bowl and mix well with a spoon.
2. Add the grated carrot to the tuna mixture and mix in.
3. Stir the raisins into the tuna mixture and mix again. Set aside.
4. Place one slice of bread on a work surface and flatten it with a rolling pin into a thin, flat piece.
5. Spread ¼ cup or less tuna mixture evenly on the flattened slice of bread.
6. Roll up the bread with tuna mixture, jelly-roll fashion. Set aside on the work surface.
7. Continue flattening and filling more bread with the tuna mixture and rolling into jelly rolls. Set all the sandwiches aside as they are completed.
8. Wrap each rolled sandwich in colored plastic wrap, twisting ends with twist-ties or colorful ribbons to resemble firecrackers.
9. Put the firecracker sandwiches on a plate or stack them in a basket to serve for a 4th of July party appetizer or lunch. Serve with ice-cold lemonade in a tall glass with red, white and blue paper napkins to brighten a happy day.

Flag Toast

Ingredients

1 slice of bread, crust removed

1 tablespoon cream cheese, softened

12 raisins

2 teaspoons jam

optional fruits or veggies for flag
　　decoration, such as peas, olives,
　　berries, bananas, chopped apple,
　　currants, golden raisins

Utensils

butter knife

cake decorator

chop stick

plate

A clean mustard or ketchup
squeeze bottle works in place of a
cake decorator, if preferred. Also, a
plastic sandwich bag with one
little corner snipped off for the
decorating point works well too.

Process

1. Place the bread in the toaster and toast just until the bread hardens. Do not brown the bread.
2. Spread the cream cheese on one side of the toast with a butter knife. Set aside.
3. Spoon jam into the cake decorator, squeeze bottle or plastic bag.
4. Squeeze stripes and designs onto the toast to resemble a flag. Flags can be of this country, other countries, or design a flag from an imaginary country, planet, club or world.
5. Decorate the toast with raisins for stars or other foods of any kind.
6. Place the flag toast on the plate.
7. Place the chop stick to the left of the flag, to represent the flag pole, and serve.

Dipped Bricks

SERVES 3 TO 8

Ingredients

1 cup semisweet-chocolate chips

bar (3 ounces) white chocolate, broken
 into small pieces

pretzel rods

suggested decorations, such as
 sprinkles, nuts, coconut, granola

Utensils

2 small microwave-safe bowls or
 saucepans

2 wooden spoons

wire cooling rack

wax paper

Process

1. Place the chocolate chips in a small microwave-safe bowl or saucepan.
2. Microwave the chocolate chips on medium for 2 minutes, then stir.
3. Take the chocolate out of the microwave and let stand about 1 minute, then stir again until smooth.
4. Place the white chocolate in another bowl. Microwave the white chocolate on medium for 2 minutes. Stir.
5. Let stand about 1 minute, then stir again until smooth.
6. Decorate each pretzel rod by dipping one end of each pretzel into either of the melted chocolates. (Or dip a pretzel into one chocolate, let it set briefly, then drizzle the other chocolate with a spoon over the first.)
7. Before the chocolate dries, sprinkle decorations onto dipped ends of pretzels.
8. Place the pretzels on a wire rack until chocolate is dry.
9. Stack the pretzel bricks on a serving platter, one on top of another as if constructing a building, before serving.

Heavenly Carrot Stars

SERVES 1 OR MORE

Ingredients

large, fat carrots

Utensils

vegetable peeler

knife and cutting board

citrus stripper

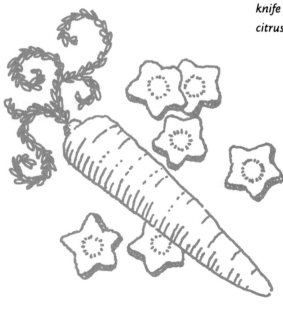

92

Process

1. Scrape a carrot with the vegetable peeler. Discard peelings.
2. Place the carrot on the cutting board.
3. Cut off the stem of the carrot. Cut off any part of the carrot that is not ½ inch in diameter and save these remaining parts or eat them as a snack.
4. Hold the carrot upright, resting on the wide flat end.
5. Use a citrus stripper to cut a thin lengthwise slice from one side of the carrot.
6. Turn the carrot a little. Hold the carrot on the wide flat end as in step 4 and repeat the thin slicing with the citrus stripper, making a second cut.
7. Continue steps 5 and 6 until a total of 5 cuts have been made. (Any number of cuts makes a design but 5 makes the traditional star shape.)
8. Place the carrot on its side. Slice the carrot to make stars.
9. Eat the stars for a raw vegetable snack, for dipping or for a garnish in salads or other recipes.

Breakfast Jelly Paint

Ingredients

smooth jelly

hot cereal, such as Cream of Wheat

fresh or canned fruits, such as banana
slices, peaches, strawberries,
berries, pears, raisins

brown sugar and milk

Utensils

clean mustard squeeze bottle

saucepan

mixing and serving spoon

serving bowls

bowls for fruit

Process

1. Fill the squeeze bottle with jelly. Set aside.
2. Prepare the cereal on the stove in a saucepan according to box directions. Most hot cereals take 10 minutes or less.
3. Spoon the warm, cooked cereal into serving bowls.
4. Serve each person a bowl of cereal. Each person can draw pictures and designs by squeezing the jelly onto the cereal.
5. Add designs and decorations with fruits of choice.
6. Serve with brown sugar and milk, if desired.

Sandwich Coins

ALLOW 1 SANDWICH PER PERSON

Ingredients

bread slices, two per person
peanut butter
honey
½ cup water in a cup
melted butter
cold milk (optional)
cup of soup per serving (optional)

Utensils

oven preheated to 350°F
spreading knife
fork
pastry brush
baking sheet
choice of tools, such as cookie cutters,
    any shape jar lids, jars with
    medium-wide mouth
oven mitts

Process

1. Cut pairs of circles from the bread with cookie cutter, lid or jar mouth.
2. Spread one circle with peanut butter. Spread the matching circle with honey. Stick the two circles together.
3. Dip the tines of the fork in water and press the tips of the tines around the edge of each sandwich to seal the peanut butter and honey inside. Press firmly, making tiny lines around the edges of the sandwich.
4. Place the sandwich cookies on the baking sheet.
5. Brush the top of each cookie with melted butter.
6. Slip the sandwich cookies into the oven and bake at 350°F for a few minutes until toasty and brown. Wearing oven mitts, remove the sandwich cookies from the oven and cool slightly before serving.

On other occasions, experiment with sandwich fillings instead of peanut butter and honey, such as tuna salad, cheese, egg salad, taco meat, jelly or jam.

Star-Studded Pizza

Ingredients

3 slices of cheese
one-half of a 3½-ounce package sliced
　　pepperoni
prepared frozen cheese pizza

Utensils

oven preheated to 375°F or according
　　to package directions
2-inch star-shaped cookie cutter
¾-inch star-shaped cookie cutter
knife
baking sheet
oven mitts

Process

1. With the 2-inch star-shaped cookie cutter, cut each slice of cheese into two stars. Or, cut them freehand with a small knife. Save the extra cheese trimmings to decorate the pizza.

2. With a ¾-inch star-shaped cookie cutter, cut a star from each slice of pepperoni.

3. Chop any pepperoni trimmings to add to the pizza later.

4. Spread the pepperoni and cheese stars over the pizza. Add any extra pepperoni or cheese trimmings.

5. Place the pizza on the baking sheet.

6. Put the pizza in the oven and bake according to package directions, usually about 20 minutes or until hot and bubbly.

7. Wear oven mitts and remove the star-studded pizza from the oven. Serve as an entree or as a party snack.

Nest in a Basket

Ingredients

3 large shredded wheat biscuits

⅓ cup shredded coconut

1½ tablespoons light brown sugar

⅓ cup butter or margarine, melted

1½ cups low-fat vanilla yogurt

2 cup grapes

lettuce leaves or sprouts (optional)

Utensils

oven preheated to 350°F

muffin tins

aluminum foil

3 to 6 salad plates

medium mixing bowl and spoon

oven mitts

Process

1. Line the muffin cups with aluminum foil, letting some foil overhang each cup. Set aside.
2. Place a lettuce leaf or large pinch of sprouts on each salad plate. Set aside.
3. Crumble the shredded wheat into the mixing bowl. Add the coconut and brown sugar to the crumbled shredded wheat and mix together with the mixing spoon.
4. Pour the melted butter over the shredded wheat mixture and mix well.
5. Press the shredded wheat mixture onto the bottom and up the sides of the muffin cups.
6. Place the muffin tin in the oven and bake for 10 minutes at 350°, or until wheat biscuit mixture is light golden brown and crisp. Wear oven mitts and remove the muffin tin from the oven. Cool for 30 minutes.
7. Remove the nests from the pans by lifting the foil by the edges. Gently peel the foil off the nest baskets.
8. Place the nest basket on a salad plate covered with lettuce or sprouts.
9. Place 2 to 3 tablespoons of yogurt in the bottom of each nest basket. Place grapes in the nest baskets on top of the yogurt to resemble eggs.

About the Authors

MARYANN F. KOHL presents workshops for teachers at early childhood conferences all over the U.S. She received her B.A. in Elementary Education from Old Dominion University in Virginia. Ms. Kohl shares her enthusiasm for learning through teaching creative art to young children, using both integrated curriculum and learning center approaches. Ms. Kohl lives with her husband in Bellingham, Washington.

MaryAnn F. Kohl's other books include *ScienceArts* with Jean Potter, *Good Earth Art* and *MathArts* with Cindy Gainer, *Discovering Great Artists* with Kim Solga, *Preschool Art, Scribble Art* and *Mudworks*. Five of her books have won Benjamin Franklin awards.

JEAN POTTER is a full-time writer. She has been a teacher and State Coordinator of Early Childhood Education in West Virginia. In 1982, she was appointed by President Ronald W. Reagan as Acting Assistant Secretary of Elementary and Secondary Education for the U.S. Department of Education. She holds a B.A from Edinboro State College and an M.A. degree from West Virginia University. She lives in Charleston, West Virginia, with her husband.

Jean Potter has written *Nature in a Nutshell, Science in Seconds, The Science of Toys, Beach Science,* and *ScienceArt.*